IMAGES
of England

BUNGAY TO BECCLES

The Falcon pub was on the corner of Sheepgate and New Market, Beccles, where Martin's newsagents' shop now is. Mr Balls was the landlord, and his brother, Mr A.J. Balls, kept the wet fish shop next door. The dogs, pictured here with the brothers in around 1910, may have belonged to the pub.

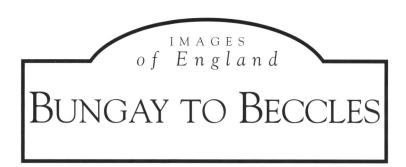

IMAGES
of England

BUNGAY TO BECCLES

Compiled by
Terry Reeve and Chris Reeve

TEMPUS

First published 1998
Reprinted 1999
Copyright © Terry and Chris Reeve, 1998

Tempus Publishing Limited
The Mill, Brimscombe Port,
Stroud, Gloucestershire, GL5 2QG

ISBN 0 7524 1177 2

Typesetting and origination by
Tempus Publishing Limited
Printed in Great Britain by
Midway Clark Printing, Wiltshire

Mothers and babies lined up for the Bungay 'Best Baby' competition, 1932. See also page 57.

Contents

Introduction   7

1. Street Scenes   9

2. Shops   25

3. Historic Buildings   35

4. Organizations   45

5. Schools   59

6. Characters   69

7. Landscape and Agriculture   79

8. Public Events and Celebrations   87

9. Railways   97

10. The River Waveney and Floods   105

11. Industry   115

A day of nostalgia at Bungay: on 5 January 1953, the Town Reeve, Mr Douglas Hewitt, shook hands with passengers as the last passenger train to run on the Waveney Valley line left Bungay station. The public were able to travel free for the sad occasion.

Introduction

Bungay and Beccles are the twin towns of the beautiful Waveney Valley, with its broad flood plain, where the River Waveney forms the border between Norfolk and Suffolk. These are two ancient towns, mentioned in the Domesday Book and steeped in history, with Beccles, the larger of the two, once a borough (its charter was granted by Elizabeth I in 1584), and Bungay now the only town in England still retaining the ancient office of Town Reeve, a title dating back to Saxon times.

Bungay, which has a population of about 5,000, is famous for its twelfth-century castle, built by Hugh Bigod, Duke of Norfolk, one of the signatories to Magna Carta, who fell out with Henry II. Its features include the Saxon parish church of Holy Trinity, the now redundant St Mary's church, many fine Georgian buildings, the Roman well and the Butter Cross, rebuilt in 1689 after the Great Fire of Bungay of 1688 destroyed most of the town.

The legend of the Black Dog of Bungay has also made the town famous, with visitors always curious to know about it. It was in August 1577 that a fierce black dog dashed into St Mary's church during a violent thunderstorm, and so frightened the congregation gathered there that two are said to have died on the spot, and two men tolling the bell in the tower also died. Church archives record only two deaths. It is a gruesome legend, but one which has made the town known far and wide.

Beccles, a town of about 11,000, is linked to the Norfolk Broads via the river Waveney. Its parish church of St Michael has its tower separated from the main body of the church, the original tower having slipped down the steep side of the valley centuries ago. It too suffered a serious fire in 1586, and other less serious fires in the seventeenth century.

Both towns are home to large book printing companies – William Clowes at Beccles, and Clays, whose slogan is 'Bookprinters to the World', at Bungay. Both are among the largest employers in the Waveney Valley.

This book attempts to reflect in old photographs something of the atmosphere of times gone by in these two fine market towns, also including a glimpse of the villages between them – Mettingham, Shipmeadow and Barsham on the Suffolk side of the valley and, on the Norfolk side, Earsham, Ditchingham, Broome, Ellingham, Geldeston and Gillingham.

A number of engravings included date back to the early nineteenth century. The photographs go back to 1859, though most are from the very early twentieth century. We are particularly indebted to the Bungay Town Recorder, Frank Honeywood, and Roy Link of Beccles, who both have extensive photographic collections, and who allowed us to draw freely on them and on their knowledge of the subjects. This work would not have been possible without their ready co-operation, and pictures from their collections form the major part of this look back at the Waveney Valley communities.

We are also grateful to a number of other people who have made photographs available, particularly Colin Buck, who has a collection of Mettingham photographs, Jean Hansey of Ditchingham, John Goldsmith of Southwold, Mrs D. Powley of Beccles, and Mrs G. Brown of Bungay.

Master Christopher Honeywood taking a donkey ride in Upper Olland Street, Bungay, in 1930. He is just passing the Gas House Lane (now Rose Lane) junction on the right. The building on the left, with chimney pots stacked at first floor level, was at the entrance to Botwright's builder's yard. It was demolished thirty years ago.

One

Street Scenes

Beccles and Bungay are similar in a number of ways, often causing visitors to confuse one with another in their recollections. Both are surrounded by water meadows and command extensive views across green pastures under the vast and ever changing East Anglian skies. Both have small market centres dominated by medieval church towers, and with fascinating, narrow side streets radiating out in all directions. The streets combine an attractive mix of commercial and residential properties, whereas in many larger towns the shopping precincts are often entirely divorced from housing areas.

Beccles no longer retains its spacious market area due to later building development, but in Bungay the centre remains little altered since its rebuilding after the great fire of 1688. The street scenes depicted in this collection are still almost immediately recognizable, but they represent a more leisurely way of life, with horse-drawn traffic, and shopkeepers chatting outside their premises to passers by. Merchandise could be displayed outside without fear of pilfering and children could play in the centre of the road without the risk of being knocked down by fast-moving traffic. It is the absence of the motor vehicle and all the street furniture connected with its use which marks the major difference between street scenes then and now.

The village of Gillingham, which borders Beccles, was on the main road to Norwich until the Beccles bypass was built. This was the scene in 1914, as the open-top bus to Loddon, on the way to Norwich, passed the Swan Inn. The bus is packed. Note that passengers sat beside the driver as well as inside the bus, in order to get as many people in as possible.

A motor omnibus at Earsham with The Street in the background, c. 1910. It could almost be the same bus as in the picture above, with passengers again seated beside the driver. Note the milestone on the left.

The scene in St Mary's Street, Bungay, *c.* 1908. The shop on the left, Whittrick's fancy repository, later became Spashett's toy shop and today is Paper Chain newsagents, still retaining the striking door pillars on either side. Next door was the shop of J. Edwards, music seller, and next to that was, and still is, Martin's the butchers.

Earsham Street, Bungay, *c.* 1900. The pump in the left foreground was a familiar and much used facility for years. It was near the Chaucer Street junction. The barber's pole on the right signifies the gents' hairdressers business which was there till the 1950s. More recently, until 1998, the premises housed a ladies' hair salon.

Blyburgate, Beccles, in 1911, with workmen busy on roadworks near the Newgate junction, probably laying new sewers.

Alexandra Road at Beccles, *c.* 1910. It was then and still is a pleasant residential road where the appearance has changed little over the years since the houses, mainly Victorian, were built.

Two ponies pulling a trap containing two ladies in Upper Olland Street, Bungay, *c*. 1900. The wooden fence borders the Honeypot Meadow, on the corner of The Folly footpath. The meadow disappeared under development during the 1950s.

This workman's horse and carriage is pictured in Flixton Road, Bungay, *c*. 1900. The houses in the background are part of St Mary's Terrace, off Southend Road, and the mill, which lost its sails in a storm in 1918, is now a private house.

There may be some people, but not many, who can remember this scene. It shows the old Beccles Post Office and Public Hall side by side in Sheepgate, with part of the King's Head Hotel just visible to the left. Both were demolished many years ago and the public shelter and gardens now occupy the scene, beside the now pedestrianized Sheepgate.

The street scene in Sheepgate, Beccles, *c.* 1910, showing the cluttered wares on sale at K. Boots. The premises are occupied today by the card shop, Occasions.

This is Stepping Hill, one of three steep, stepped paths linking Ballygate at Beccles with Puddingmoor, which is almost at river level. The costumes of those pictured near the foot of the steps indicates that this picture was probably taken in the 1890s.

The famous charabancs, loaded with passengers eager to enjoy a day's outing from Beccles. This picture was taken outside the Bear and Bells pub in Old Market in the 1920s. Sammy Crisp, who ran the barber's shop which can just be seen in the background, was a well known character who used to run a Slate Club, with people paying in money each week which went towards the cost of the outing. On this occasion they could have been heading for Yarmouth, or further afield.

New Market, Beccles, *c.* 1865, with the King's Head straight ahead. Children are gathered around the old pump, which was pulled down in 1879 because the water was unfit to drink. Note the pram (possibly a doll's pram) pulled by one of the children.

The north side of Bungay Market Place in 1905, with the Queen's Head pub, now the National Westminster Bank, on the corner of Bridge Street, and the post office on the opposite corner in premises now occupied by Abbott's estate agents.

Station Road, Bungay, in 1906, with the Victorian Waveney Terrace prominent. The road is now known as Outney Road, its name before Bungay railway station, to which it gave access, was built. The white house in the middle distance is the former Cherry Tree pub.

Geldeston is a small village but even today it boasts two pubs. This is the Wherry, in The Street, in 1935. It has changed much since this time and attracts customers from a wide area. The other Geldeston pub is the Locks inn.

The Star Hotel, on the corner of Station Road and Gosford Road, *c.* 1910. The sign clearly shows it as a commercial and family hotel, and it was highly popular at its advantageous position close to the railway station. The landlord of the day was Mr G.W. Jupp. Sadly, the Star closed recently (in 1998).

A pre-First World War view of the centre of Beccles with the familiar detached tower of St Michael's church prominent. The building partly seen on the left was occupied on the first floor by the offices of the *East Suffolk Gazette* and on the ground floor by a fruiterer and seedsman. Further along is the ironmongery business of Masters (in premises now occupied by Superdrug). It later became Masters and Skevens and moved across the road further down The Walk. On the right-hand corner can be seen McQueen's outfitters, hatters, hosiers and glovers shop.

A busy scene at New Market, Beccles, around the turn of the century. T.J. Self, fruiterer and seedsman, obviously occupied a busy corner of the area, and the picture is a good illustration of the men's and women's fashions of the time. The premises above the shop were occupied at the time by the offices of the *East Suffolk Gazette*. Until recently, Self's premises housed the Beccles branch of Peatling and Cawdron.

Bungay town centre, around 1900, with W A Gilbey's wine and spirits store in the left centre, where the Norwich and Peterborough Building Society offices now are, and the King's Head hotel on the right. Note the horse carts parked on their sides under the Butter Cross. The roof lines have hardly changed at all, though the three tall chimney stacks on the right centre have been demolished.

Bridge Street, Bungay, c. 1920. The horse and cart has just passed the Chequers public house on the right, once one of several pubs in the street, but today the only one. Coe's grocer's shop, in the right foreground, is now a private house.

This fine view of Exchange Square, Beccles, in around 1910 shows clearly the former Gun and Hill Sheffield warehouse, where the Suffolk House florist now is and, in the centre background, the Star Supply Stores. Those premises are now occupied by Grey's opticians, with the basement of it forming the popular Old Wine Vaults restaurant.

This rare picture of the imposing – and, to those about to become inmates, no doubt daunting – entrance to Beccles Gaol, as it was in 1895. The prison ceased to be used in the early part of this century and was demolished in about 1960, but the road leading of the main entrance to William Clowes' book printing factory is still called Gaol Lane.

St John's Road, Bungay, in 1905. The carriage-making and repairing premises on the right are now part of R. Charlish's garage and show room. Further along, at the Southend Road junction, is part of what is now the Three Willows Garden Centre site.

A horse and cart makes its way down Flixton Road, Bungay, *c.* 1930. It was previously known as Grove Road. Note the gas lamps, and the vent pipes to the sewerage system.

London Road, Beccles, in the beauty of the winter of 1896 following a heavy snowfall, with the tracks of carts clearly visible.

Priory Road in Beccles, before 1914, seen from the tower of St Benet's Roman Catholic church. In the foreground is the area which is now Grange Road and Upper Grange Road. The windmill in the background would have been close to London Road.

A horse-drawn hearse makes its way through Bungay town centre in 1930, followed by mourners in carriages, probably on their way to St Mary's church for the funeral service for Mr Hancy. The undertaker, walking ahead of the cortège on the right, was Mr Alfred Biles.

A peaceful scene in Gillingham around the turn of the century, with a horse-drawn cart passing the original Swan inn on its way over Gillingham Dam to Beccles, and perhaps to market.

Two

Shops

Whereas many towns are now dominated by large chain stores and shopping centres, Bungay and Beccles both retain a number of small, privately owned businesses. These continue to provide a personal and friendly service, some of the businesses dating back to the last century or earlier. In Bungay, Nursey and Son, the sheepskin specialist, was established in 1790, while Wightman's family drapery and furniture store has been in the Market Place since the mid-nineteenth century.

The variety of merchandise which these small shops can offer means that there is still no need to shop outside the town. You can still enjoy a leisurely stroll from the greengrocer's to the baker's and the chemist's, savouring all the delightful smells which characterize their wares, and pause for a gossip with the shop assistants and the other customers whom you grow used to meeting there. This relaxed and friendly atmosphere is even more noticeable in the smaller Waveney Valley villages, where the main streets still feature the single village shop, the post office and pub, just as they did a century ago.

The shopping areas in Bungay and Beccles have changed little during this century. The main difference is that the milliners, saddlers and blacksmiths have been replaced by shops selling antiques, videos or charity merchandise, reflecting the changes in lifestyle during the later twentieth century.

An example of how as many items as possible were displayed prominently to the public by tradesmen. This is the shop of bootmakers and repairers W.H. Sturgess in St Mary's Street, Bungay, in around 1900. Mr Sturgess, who made stylish boots on the premises, could be the man in the horse and trap, with two young children. Today these premises belong to jewellers Robert Meadley. Coincidentally, when this picture was taken the shop next door was that of R.W. Bishop, selling jewellery and watches.

A hostelry familiar to river-borne visitors to Beccles is the Ship Inn, standing by Beccles Bridge at the entrance to the town from Gillingham. Its licensee in around 1910, when this picture was taken, was Arthur Woolner. Today it is a guest house and restaurant.

Turner's Alehouse was in Hungate, Beccles, where the Chicken 2000 takeaway now is. The picture was taken in around 1900 and shows the proprietor or assistant standing in the doorway with a tradesman's basket. Note the man with the handcart on the right, and the man in a bowler hat to the left.

This premises of J.W. Frost, authorized waterworks and sanitary plumber, was in Ballygate, Beccles, and is pictured here around 1900.

The Co-operative Society had, and still has, extensive premises in Smallgate, Beccles. Here the staff of the confectionery department are pictured outside in 1913.

These young ladies were pictured in 1916 when all were on the staff of the Beccles Co-operative Society, which had its premises in Smallgate. The gentleman in the back row is believed to be the manager.

A general view of the Co-operative Society premises in Smallgate, Beccles, with staff and onlookers gathered outside the new extension, built shortly before the First World War.

New Market, Beccles, around the turn of the century, with Stead and Simpson's shoe shop on the left, next door to the King's Head Hotel, and the Falcon Inn in the background, where Martin's the newsagents now trades.

A marvellous display of fish and game at the premises of Paddle's in Smallgate, Beccles, *c.* 1910. Mr Paddle, in the bowler hat on the left, styled his business the 'Little Billingsgate Fish Emporium', but he clearly also sold duck and rabbit, and probably other game. He was a well known character in the town.

The International Stores' premises in Beccles town centre in the early 1920s, with the staff posing outside. Note the shining white linen overalls, and the hand delivery cart on the left.

Morling's Music Centre is still a prominent and successful business in New Market in the centre of Beccles. This picture of it, from in the 1920s, shows one of the Morling family, Miss Morling, on the left, with the shop assistant, Miss Dorling, on the right. In the centre is the shop manager at the time, Mr Barber.

In 1910, when this picture was taken, the horse was still the main mode of transport and saddleries did a roaring trade. This one, Branford's, was in Blyburgate, and demonstrates how shopkeepers put as many wares as possible on show to passers by. The shop has had many uses in recent years; it was Crisp's newsagents for some time, and is now 'Deja Vu' clothes shop.

C.S. Sampson's family butcher's shop was situated in Denmark Road, Beccles. This picture, taken in 1908, shows Mr Sampson himself in the doorway, with his son, young Jimmy Sampson, no doubt learning the trade at the time, on the left. The impressive display of prize-winning meat is obviously the result of a trade show of some kind.

G.W. Chase had his butcher's shop in Trinity Street, Bungay, in premises now occupied by the National Westminster Bank. The picture was taken on 6 January 1920 and the greetings sign from the Christmas just past is still in position. It was normal for carcasses to be hung outside in this way, and at that time of year it was probably cold enough not to matter, though modern day health inspectors would turn white! The man standing second from right is Mr E. Snelling.

W. Patrick's shop on the corner of Popson Street and Chaucer Street, Bungay, c. 1930. Later Brill's shop, it was demolished, along with other houses on the west side of the street, in 1982 for road widening in conjunction with the Bungay bypass scheme. One of the posters on the side of the shop is for the Electric Theatre, Bungay.

Gillingham is a small village which today still retains most village facilities – church, school, pub and village hall. Sadly its village shop and post office has closed and is now a hair salon, but this picture taken soon after the turn of the century shows the shop in The Street when it was a focal point of the community.

Beccles Post Office in Sheepgate, c. 1910, with a horse and cart standing outside. The bank on the left is now Lloyds Bank.

Three
Historic Buildings

For a town of its size, Bungay has an outstanding group of ancient buildings. Due to its strong defensive position on high ground virtually encircled by the River Waveney, it attracted settlers from prehistoric times. By the eleventh century it was recorded in Domesday Book as a town of importance. Roman remains are thought to include the Borough Well, while the Saxons contributed the surviving defensive earthworks and were probably responsible for the building of Holy Trinity church in around 1040. Hugh Bigod erected his powerful Norman keep around 1170, and in the medieval period the Benedictine Priory and the graceful structure of St Mary's church were created.

However, both Bungay and Beccles are chiefly characterized by a varied range of Georgian buildings. These mellowed red brick properties with broad façades highlighted by elegant porticoes are apparent throughout the town centres and in the side streets. In some cases Victorian and later alterations have been made, notably to the shop fronts, creating a not unpleasant array of architectural styles. Bungay also retains its Butter Cross, which was rebuilt after the fire of 1688, surmounted by the superb eighteenth-century figure of Justice.

Other notable buildings in the Beccles area include the medieval bell tower of St Michael's and the seventeenth-century Sir John Leman School, recently converted to use as a museum. Further along the Waveney Valley can be seen the ruins of Mettingham Castle and the remains of various mill towers remind us of the previous prosperity of milling as an industry.

An engraving of Mettingham Castle, of the late eighteenth century. This entrance is still there today as part of the remains of the castle, which was part of a college in the fifteenth century.

THE WEST VIEW OF BUNGAY CASTLE, IN THE COUNTY OF SUFFOLK.

To the Right Honourable
William Henry Earl of Rochford
This Prospect is humbly Inscribd by his Lordships
most Obedient Serv.t
Jas.r Kirby

This Castle stands upon the Banks of the River Waveney supposd to have been built by the Bigods Earls of Norfolk Notwithstanding its present ruinous Condition. Hugh Bigod in the Reign of K.: Stephen boasted of it as a place impregnable.

Drawn by Ja.s Kirby & Publishd by him 25. March 1748. — Engravd by J. Wood.

This engraving of Bungay Castle is dated 1748, and shows the house built between the gate towers of the keep, the ruins of which can clearly be seen. Note the cottages on the right, thrown up against the castle walls. The castle was built by the Bigods in around 1170, was later largely destroyed and rebuilt in 1294 by Roger Bigod.

The peal of bells which hangs in the detached tower of St Michael's church, Beccles. On this occasion they had probably been taken down for recasting, and the names on the bells probably correspond with the gentlemen in the picture, taken in about 1910. They are the Rector of Beccles, the Revd John Rowsell; Mr A.R. Clatworthy, churchwarden; Womack Brooks, churchwarden; Henry Hopson, bell-ringing captain; and the Mayor of Beccles, Mr K.R. Money.

The Lecture Hall was an imposing building constructed in 1804 in Fair Close, Beccles, and for a long time was a popular meeting place and library for those interested in furthering their education. Earlier this century it became the Co-operative Society dairy from where milkmen delivered around the town and district. It was eventually demolished in May 1998, some years after it ceased being used as a dairy.

The Elizabethan Roos Hall, beside Bungay Road, Beccles, with ornamental gardens and lawns in the foreground, before 1914.

Broome Place, Broome, *c.* 1900. At this time it was the home of the De Poix family, who ran a thriving fruit farm and arable farm in the village. Local people, and schoolboys in the summer holidays, were employed picking apples in the extensive orchards.

A splendid view of the imposing Flixton Hall, near Bungay, in around 1920, with guests gathered, perhaps for a social event or dinner party. The family seat of the Adairs in the nineteenth and early twentieth centuries, the hall was commandeered as military headquarters during the Second World War. It was demolished in the 1950s for tax reasons.

The Butter Cross, Bungay, c. 1900, showing a group of children perhaps waiting for horse-drawn transport. Note the cart parked on end under the Butter Cross. It was built in 1689 in the Market Place to replace one on the site destroyed in the Great Fire of Bungay in 1688. The figure of Justice was placed on top in 1754.

The Thatched House at Bungay, once one of the town's most attractive pubs. It was situated near the crossroads leading to Flixton and to Ilketshall St Margaret's, near the corner of St Margaret's Road. The landlord in 1900 was James Westgate, who was also a cattle dealer. Later, in 1916, Kelly's Directory names Mrs C. Catherine Mennell as the occupant. The building was demolished in the 1920s.

The Falcon Inn, just on the Norfolk side of the River Waveney outside Bungay, as it was around the turn of the century. The unmade road at the start of Ditchingham Dam is clearly visible. Thomas B. Wilson was landlord at the time, and the pub sign advertises Bullard and Son's superior ales.

The Buck Inn at Flixton, *c.* 1915. Standing beside what is now the B1062 road three miles outside Bungay, it has long been a popular venue and was once run by singer Alan Breeze, who sang with Billy Cotton's band on radio and television shows. At the end of the nineteenth century the building was a farmhouse, occupied by the Wilson family.

Cottages on the corner of Rectory Lane, Worlingham, *c.* 1900. They had to be demolished in the 1970s to improve visibility on to the Lowestoft Road.

Barsham parish church, between Beccles and Bungay, in 1904. Note its round Saxon tower, and the unique criss-cross pattern of its east window, just visible.

Holy Trinity church, Bungay, c. 1900. The Saxon tower has been dated at around 1041, with the nave added about 100 years later. The dormer window in the roof was created in Victorian times to light the organ loft when the organ was installed. The church is now Bungay's parish church.

Beccles War Memorial in St Mary's Road, with the War Memorial Hospital, opened in 1924, in the background. It has been extended considerably since this picture was taken and is now a busy community hospital, managed by the Allington NHS Trust.

The Castle Hills at Bungay on 24 July 1903, with the tower of St Mary's Church rising in the background, and the rooftops of premises on the west side of St Mary's Street just visible beyond the hills. The picture was taken from the marshes, and Castle Lane runs through the middle of this picture on the photographer's side of the hills. It shows just how effective they must have been as a defence in medieval times.

St Mary's church, Bungay, a Waveney Valley landmark. Standing in the centre of the town, it dates back to the thirteenth century, and was badly damaged in the great fire of 1688. The south aisle roof and the top half of the tower had to be completely rebuilt, and it finally re-opened in 1699. The church became redundant in 1979 and is now cared for by the Churches Conservation Trust and the Friends of St Mary's.

Four

Organizations

Town and village clubs, societies and groups have always been a strong point in the Waveney Valley. This section reflects some of them, from wartime to peacetime, and from civic to volunteer organizations. Beccles was a borough until local government reorganization in 1974. Bungay was administered by the ancient Bungay Town Trust until the Urban District Council was formed in 1910, and is the only place in the country to retain the ancient office of Town Reeve. He or she heads the Town Trust which still runs the weekly market, almshouses and the Borough Well, and is responsible for the Castle Hills and various town lands. Both towns have been headed by town councils since 1974, while villages have retained their parish councils or parish meetings. Church organizations, of course, have also played a prominent part in community life for centuries.

The post-war Welfare Foods campaign in the eastern region was promoted in Bungay on 19 February 1952, at the Trinity Rooms, with these babies in arms enjoying pure orange juice. The Town Reeve that year, John Clay, is seated in the front row with a baby on his knee; Mrs W.M. Lummis, wife of the Vicar of Bungay and a member of the Bungay Food Control Committee, is at the back on the left; and Mr Ronald Wightman, chairman of the committee, is at the back on the right.

The annual Bungay Town Dinner, hosted by the Town Reeve, was – and still is – Bungay's premier social occasion. The tradition was revived in 1934 by Dr Leonard Cane, and the picture here was taken in 1958 at the King's Head hotel ballroom when his son, Dr Hugh Cane, held the unique and historic office. He can be seen by the candelabra with his wife, Margaret.

The men of the Beccles Home Guard in the 1940s. It was a large brigade and its commanding officer was Col. Chandos of Worlingham Hall, who is pictured sitting in the front row with a stick. This may have been a district gathering, as some members of the Bungay Home Guard are among this contingent. The Home Guard remained active for some years after the end of the Second World War.

The Beccles Militia was a group of men who got together under that name during Victorian times, and are pictured here c. 1860. They were all volunteers and their role appears to have been peaceful. T.P. Angel, who was in the army at the time, may have been the corps' captain or commander in his spare time.

The Beccles area police force lined up for the camera outside the police station, which in the first part of the century was at the back of William Clowes Ltd's factory, near the gaol in Gaol Lane. The police station was pulled down in the 1920s, when the force moved to the one in London Road which is still in use today, though the number of officers based there is considerably smaller.

Bungay's first mobile fire engine and tender, a Daimler, outside the Methodist church in Trinity Street, opposite its station in Cross Street, in the late 1920s. The firemen, from left to right, are: J. Wilson (driver), Charles Bedwell (captain), Major Read, Charlie Pettitt, Harry Watson, Alf Ambrose, Will Burton, Edgar Bedwell, George Butcher, Sid Larke.

Every town had its Home Guard unit during the Second World War. This is the Bungay unit, pictured in front of Bungay Castle, with Douglas Hewitt, its commander and headmaster at Bungay Grammar School, pictured fifth from the right. Sixth from the right is G. Powell, the school's science master, and fourth from the right Walter Reeve, uncle of the compilers of this book.

Bungay's wartime rescue team at the rear of the Fleece Hotel in St Mary's Street in the 1940s. They were assembled to go into action in the event of a bomb strike on the town.

The workhouse at Shipmeadow, between Beccles and Bungay, was opened in the second half of the eighteenth century and remained in use for the poor and homeless until the 1930s. This picture of a group of the inmates outside the H-shaped building was taken in around 1910.

Another group at the Shipmeadow workhouse, which stood in a prominent position overlooking the Waveney Valley. These were probably members of staff there, and are pictured with T.P. Angel, a prominent Beccles businessman who lived in Northgate, and was probably chairman of the board of guardians. Both pictures on this page came from his family album.

The Wesleyan chapel in Beccles stood in Station Road. As can be seen from the banner, this picture of its Band of Hope was taken in 1902. Those pictured were the prominent members of the chapel.

Mettingham Mothers' Union members with their children outside the Church Rooms in Vicarage Lane, c. 1930. The style of the ladies' hats gives a clue as to the date.

Members of the local Young Farmers' Club at Beccles Livestock Market in the 1930s, with local farmers and auctioneers. Mr F.A. Grimmer is fifth from the left.

Outside the Tally Ho! pub at Mettingham, *c*. 1930. These villagers are about to board the Eastern Counties bus, behind them.

This local dance band was popular in the Waveney Valley in the 1950s, when this picture was taken. Usually known as the Ivor Quartet, they played at dances at local village halls, and the venue here may have been the former St John Ambulance Brigade headquarters, which was in a nissen hut at the Honeypot Meadow in Bardolph Road, Bungay, at the time. The chap playing the saxophone, on the left in the band, was the late Mr Vivian Palmer, Derek Kenyon is on drums and Ivor Wigg, who doubled on the accordion, is playing the trumpet.

The Beccles Institute Bowls Club was formed in the early part of this century and continues until this day. It had, and still has, its green at Fair Close, to the rear of the library at Beccles, and fields teams in the Beccles and District Bowls League and other competitions. This picture shows members of the club at the green in 1921.

The Bungay Athletics Club Challenge Shield was competed for annually at a variety of athletic and other sporting events. These two men were the winners in 1893, with Sid Charlish the one with the bicycle on the right.

Several boxing shows were staged by promoter Cliff Butler in Bungay before and after the Second World War, on the field which was behind the White Lion Hotel in Earsham Street. He brought top names to the town, as can be seen from this bill for 4 August 1949 topped by Lee Savold, then America's chief contender for the world heavyweight championship.

A Mothering Sunday group outside the vicarage at Mettingham, *c*. 1920. The vicar's wife, Mrs Davis, is the lady in the dark hat standing at the back, while second from the right in the front row is Eva Coe.

Members of the Mettingham church Sunday school, pictured at New Road in the early 1950s, with the girls in berets or bonnets and the boys bare-headed.

Members of Beccles Girl Guides company, pictured in the town *c*. 1910. The date is given away by the uniforms, particularly the hats, which are a far cry from the styles of headgear worn by Guides today. The Brownies are seated at the front.

The Bungay No. 4 Company Army Cadet Force band and cadets parading through Broad Street in 1947. The two young cyclists on the right are passing what was for many years Bungay's library, until the new one was opened in 1993, in Wharton Street.

The Mothers' Union movement was at its height in the years between the two world wars, with groups attached to churches having many members. This picture shows the Beccles Mothers' Union annual Christmas party at the St Michael's church rooms in Ballygate, in 1938. Today the building is a private residence.

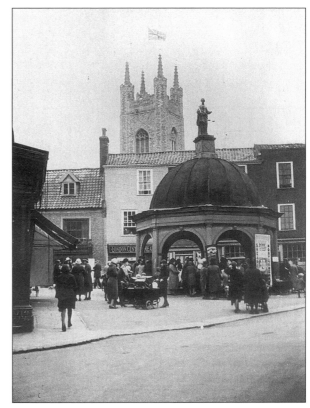

Mothers and children gather for a Bungay Baby Welfare Centre 'Best Baby' competition at the Butter Cross, Bungay, 1932. The picture on page 4 of this book was taken on the same occasion. Note the uniform style and rather sombre colours of the prams.

United Friendly Societies

A
CONCERT

UNDER THE PATRONAGE OF THE TOWN REEVE
WILL BE GIVEN

In Aid of the Ditchingham Hospital Jubilee Fund

On TUESDAY, OCTOBER 30th, 1923

AT THE

CHAUCER INSTITUTE

ARTISTES:
Mr. H. J. MARTIN (Humorist)
Messrs. R. HAMMOND, H. CHILVERS, H. C. CHASE, H. STONE and J. E. CLARKE.

CONCLUDING WITH

A LAUGHABLE SKETCH

ENTITLED

"OLD BACHELORS MATCHED"

Selections by Mr. Honeywood's Band.

Doors open at 7.30.   Commence at 8.
Prices of Admission: Front Seats, 2/-; Second Seats, 1/-

Tickets can be obtained H. W. SHORT'S, Market Place, Bungay.

As the Chaucer Institute has been lent for the occasion the entire takings will be given to the above fund.

A poster for a concert staged by the United Friendly Societies in 1923 to raise funds for All Hallows Hospital at Ditchingham. Bungay has always given great support to that hospital and today much of the fundraising is carried out by the Friends of All Hallows under the committed chairmanship of Mr Harald Pulford. The Chaucer Institute, where this concert was held, was built in 1909 as a library and recreational and cultural club for employees of book printers Richard Clay Ltd, and was a favourite venue for concerts and plays for many years.

Five

Schools

From the late nineteenth century, almost every village had its school, and that was the case with those along the Waveney Valley. In the towns of Beccles and Bungay, grammar school education had been available for centuries before that, at Bungay Grammar School and the Sir John Leman School, Beccles. Both towns also had their board schools, or national schools, which today have evolved into primary and middle schools, with the former grammar schools now comprehensive high schools; the Sir John Leman has around 1,200 pupils and Bungay High School nearly 1,000. Many village schools have closed over more recent years but memories of them, as with schools still existing, are retained through photographs. In many cases these former village schools have been converted to private homes, community halls or other community or even business uses.

The village school at Ditchingham stood in Station Road, beside All Hallows' Hospital, and served the village for nearly a century, until the new school was built at Rider Haggard Way in the 1970s. The building was demolished in the early 1990s. This picture of pupils in Class I was taken in the 1920s, and shows thirty-six children, with a man on the right, who was probably the headmaster.

Another picture of pupils at Ditchingham School, this time of thirty pupils of group I, in 1922. Note the smocks worn by some of the girls, and the leather boots worn by both sexes.

This is the old national school at Beccles, once situated in Ravensmere, where the present fire station stands. On this occasion, around 1912, it was being visited by the board of governors of the school, who included the Mayor of Beccles, seen wearing his chain of office.

St Mary's Grammar School at Beccles. This is a woodcut of the school, made in about 1890. It stood in St Mary's Road and was a private school which finally closed in the early part of this century.

Ravensmere School at Beccles had many pupils in the early part of the century. This picture of Group IV was taken in around 1917, with one of the pupils, Florence Hembling, identified third from the left. The school and building still remain today, the smallest of three primary schools in the town. During the 1980s its numbers dropped to twenty-six and it faced possible closure, but still survives, and numbers are now double that.

The Victorian Broome village school, c. 1930, with the curious pupils looking at the photographer. The building, on the corner of Sun Road, is now a guest house. It is worth noting that schools built during the Victorian period were often of similar design, complete with small bell tower.

This fine aerial view of Bungay Primary School was taken in July 1928. It was opened in 1877 in Wingfield Street and the buildings seen here are little changed. The site was later extended on to the allotments seen at the rear to provide a playing field. A two-storey block of classrooms was added in 1959, and a further six classrooms and other facilities in 1994. In this picture, the gardens and pond at the Wingfield Street frontage of the school had not yet been developed.

Wingfield Street, Bungay, c. 1920. These children were probably on their way to or from the Bungay Board School, now Bungay Primary School, a short way up the street behind the photographer.

Boys of Bungay Grammar School, pictured in 1911 in the days when the school was in Earsham Street, where the post office now is. Headmaster Mr Gardiner is standing on the right with his dog, Jim. Teacher Mr Fiske is standing on the left, and the old gentleman seated is Mr Gardiner, known to the boys as Daddy Gardiner and presumably father of the headmaster. The school moved to a new building in St John's Road in 1925.

These are the boys of Brewer's School, which was situated in what is now Wharton House in Wharton Street, Bungay. The gentleman in the long beard and hat is Sydney Brewer, headmaster at the school. The picture dates from around 1900.

An aerial view of Bungay Secondary Modern School (now Bungay Middle School) in the 1950s. It was built in 1939 as Bungay Area School.

An aerial view of Bungay Grammar School in St John's Road, *c.* 1940. The school allotments are clearly visible in the foreground, and the air-raid shelters to the left. The logs on the field to the left are laid out for seasoning by cricket bat specialist Edgar Watts Ltd. That field is now the Tower Mill housing estate.

This Bungay Council School group is pictured in 1930 with the Crabbe and Bigod Shield. The school, in Wingfield Street, is now Bungay Primary School and has over 300 children. Pictured here are: from left to right, back row: Claude Hood, Maurice Lawn (also known as Peter Dickerson), Gordon Pettitt, Peggy Smith, Grace Castleton, Olive Holland, Maud Fewtrell, Dora Gray, Harry Clarke, Fred George, Stanley Balls. Second row: Mary Whyte, ? Preston, Queenie Tillett, Vera Cooke, Phyllis Burroughs, Irene Plackett, Joyce Ling, Flo Freakes, Mollie Knights, Mary Day, Sidney Myall. Front row: Harold Messenger, Sid Larke, Bobby Cooke, Arthur Jermy, Albert Jermy, Alec Baldry.

This was Bungay Grammar School, situated in Earsham Street where the post office now is. When it was rebuilt after the Great Fire of Bungay (1688) a stone plaque recording the incident in Latin was placed in the wall. The plaque was transferred to the new building when it was built in 1925 in St John Road, and again when a new grammar school (now Bungay High School) was built at Queens Road in 1961.

Boys presenting a display of team acrobatics at the Sir John Leman Grammar School at Beccles during sports day, *c.* 1920, probably on the Ringsfield Road playing fields. This photograph was given by Miss Pye, now aged nearly ninety, and daughter of the former Mayor of Beccles, Mr Albert Pye.

The village school at Gillingham in 1936, showing a group of its pupils. This Victorian school building situated at Gillingham Dam closed in the late 1970s and has now been converted to a private house. The present school which replaced it, Gillingham St Michael Junior and Infants' School, is situated at The Boundaries, off Geldeston Road.

Gillingham's original school was an attractive Victorian building typical of many in Norfolk and North Suffolk, with its neat entrance porch. In this picture taken around 1900, note the little bell tower on the top, with the bell with which children were summoned to school. It was sited at Gillingham Dam, close to the centre of the village, and close to the blacksmith's forge, also to be seen in this picture. No doubt children tarried there to see the sparks flying from the forge and the farrier at work, busy helping to keep the many farm horses shod.

Six

Characters

All towns and villages have their local characters – those known affectionately to most of the community, who always greet them cheerily. There have been many characters around the Waveney Valley over the centuries, and this section focuses on just a few of them, from Fiddler George at Beccles to the delivery roundsmen of Bungay who were always ready for a chat when they delivered the bread, milk, butter or vegetables to customers' doors. Such roundsmen are now largely a thing of the past, with milk now virtually the only commodity still delivered regularly to the door each day.

This Co-operative Society bread cart was a familiar site around Beccles. This picture was taken around 1919 in the area to the rear of Gosford Road. Standing proudly by it is roundsman Mr Lewis, whose son used to work for the local undertaker of the day, Mr Reynolds.

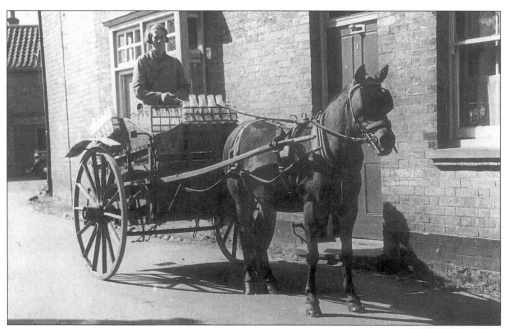

Elsie Rattle was a familiar face on many doorsteps of Bungay and district as she delivered milk – fresh and unpasteurized – for Hancy's in this pony and cart during and after the Second World War. Here she is in Chaucer Street, c. 1940.

Susan Pipe, a well known character seen around Beccles in the early 1900s, selling her wares in all areas of the community. She was known to the younger members of the community as the ragged 'bag lady'.

The sound of the strings of Fiddler George was a familiar one around the streets and roads of Beccles in the years between the two world wars, and after the Second World War. He was George Reynolds, a tramp who spent most of his time 'living rough'. His playing may not always have been tuneful, but he was a town character held in great affection up to the time of his death in about 1960. He is seen here playing at the Puddingmoor end of Stepping Hill, accompanied by his companion, Hilda Woolnough.

Porky Ward used to have his smoke house at Bridge Street, Bungay, where he did brisk business daily in the early part of this century. He is seen here on the right, with the kippers hung in neat rows, and with many hands to help him in the work.

This is Professor Rosalia, who toured the country with his Punch and Judy show, appearing before the aristocracy as well as those on holiday at places such as Yarmouth around the turn of the century. Bungay was his home town, however; he lived in Bridge Street. Children enjoyed his popular shows. This picture is thought to have been taken in Outney Road.

Carting was a regular trade in days gone by and Mr Gray, pictured here with his horse and cart, was a carter and a local character in Beccles. The picture was taken outside the Red Cow pub in Ingate, which was next door to the present Ingate pub, in around 1910. As can be seen, the Red Cow sold newspapers and the beer of the Colchester Brewing Company.

George Bowes, a Bungay baker, delivering bread in his horse and trap to a country area just outside Bungay. He had his shop at 48 Broad Street, and it was later taken over by another baker, Eastaugh. Judging by his fine horse and cart, Bowes was a prosperous tradesman.

For forty-one years Arthur Fairweather was a wood merchant in Beccles, a familiar sight around the town with his horse and cart as he delivered firewood during the 1920s and 1930s, a period in which almost every house burned wood and coal on an open fire. This picture was taken in 1930 in Newgate, at the wood yard sited where the basket shop and picture framing business now is, just as he and his horse, Duke, were about to set off with another load. Clowes' printing works is in the background, with a gas street lamp fixed to the wall.

Two well known Bungay characters of the present century, pictured on a tandem in Broad Street, c. 1960. Sid Read, at the front, was landlord of the Horse and Groom pub (now the Green Dragon) in Broad Street, and Arthur Eastaugh, at the back, ran the baker's business which had shops in Broad Street (pictured in the background) and Earsham Street.

During wartime, women took on the roles of men called to war. Here Bessie Daniels (now Bessie Taylor) is pictured with her delivery cart outside Patrick's shop in Popson Street, Bungay, in 1943. With her is Mary Reeve, who became a GI bride and emigrated to America with her husband. She is the cousin of the compilers of this book.

Miss Fenn, on crutches, pictured outside her family butcher's shop in Northgate, Beccles, where she used to take in washing and ironing as a business, no doubt at competitive rates. With her in this picture from around 1900 is her mother, Mrs Fenn.

William Rolfe, the self-styled 'King of the Norfolk Poachers', who had close connections with Mettingham. He was at his height in the early part of the century and was so famous – or notorious – that Lilias Rider Haggard compiled a biography of him entitled *I Walked by Night*.

Mr John (Broomy) Baldry was Bungay Common's bailiff during the years between the wars and was popular with children, who often ribbed him and played jokes on him. In this picture his young passenger on the horse-drawn hay rake was Master Swann.

Charles Bedwell was a well-known Bungay builder. He is pictured here in Boyscott Lane with a pony in 1888, with the row of cottages behind him still there today. At the back, right, can be seen part of what was then the Congregational church hall.

This picture was taken at the rear of the Swan Inn at Bungay, in 1903, following the Bungay pony and galloway race meeting on Outney Common. Races, including point to point, were regularly held there until 1957. Astride the horse with the trophy he won is Mr A. Read, a local hay dealer, and holding the reins is another familiar Bungay character of the day, Mr Page.

Seven

Landscape and Agriculture

The landscape of the Waveney Valley is one of its joys, and agriculture is still an industry carried on widely within that landscape. Both Beccles and Bungay stand overlooking the valley and its wide flood plain, and those who have walked the footpaths or cycled the roads in the district will testify to the fact that this area in the heart of East Anglia is not as flat as many outsiders believe.

Farming is still an important part of life in this part of the country. Farmers still have large herds of dairy cattle or bullocks for fattening, and farm many acres of arable land, with wheat, barley and oats or root crops such as potatoes, turnips and, particularly, sugar beet.

The valley has some beautiful areas, particularly the 400-acre Outney Common at Bungay, and Beccles Common, while both towns in themselves are a picturesque sight, dominated by their respective church towers, on their prominent positions for travellers approaching them. The villages, too, are attractive features of the Waveney scene.

This engraving of the Bungay landscape from the approach from Earsham was published in 1818. The drawing was by J.S. Cotman, who used a certain amount of artistic licence.

This fine picture of higgledy-piggledy rooftops in Beccles was taken from the top of St Michael's church tower in around 1910, with New Market, the Falcon Inn and the King's Head Hotel in the foreground. The large, long, factory-like building in the middle of the picture was in fact Beccles Corn Exchange, a building which for many years has been the home of Lloyds Bank.

Fruit picking has always been the source of seasonal work in the orchards and fields of the Waveney Valley, either as hourly-paid or piece work. Blackcurrants, raspberries, apples, plums, pears, runner beans – many are the crops to be gleaned. Today, much of it is done on a DIY basis. Around ninety years ago it was probably piece work for this team, about to set off on their bicycles from the Old Market, Beccles, to the strawberry fields on either side of the River Waveney, having been recruited by the farmer.

Farm labourers, with a variety of implements and a variety of hats, pictured in the fields at Broome. In the background is a horse-drawn rake, and the hall at the top of the rise in the field behind is Broome Place, home of the De Poix family.

Castle Farm at Beccles, named because of its distinctive round tower accommodation to which the more conventional house was later attached. The farmhouse has long since been demolished, but it is still remembered in the road name Castle Hill – the farm was situated on prominent high ground on the southern edge of the town. At the time this picture was taken the farm was occupied by a man called Rankin, who bred Shetland sheep dogs.

These imposing gates were erected at the end of the Avenue at Beccles, where it opens on to the Common, in around 1860, and are still there today. This woodcut of them shows them in fine condition, and was probably made soon after they were built.

This picture, of around 1900, shows the mill standing at the bottom of Southend Road, Bungay, before it lost its sails in a storm in 1918, after which it was converted to a house, its use today. The gable end in the middle of the picture is St Mary's Terrace, beside the Ups-and-Downs footpath, hidden by the hedge, which links to Hillside Road.

The view from the top of St Mary's church, Bungay, looking north over the rooftops to Outney Common, completely covered with flood water in the 1912 floods as the Waveney burst its banks. The Three Tuns Hotel can be seen in the centre foreground.

This playground, pictured in the early 1950s, was beside the Ups-and-Downs footpath which links Southend Road and Hillside Road, Bungay, and was well used by children in the Jubilee Road, Flixton Road and Hillside Road area. As well as these swings it had a roundabout, slide, seesaw, swing bars and a sandpit. It is now the Pennyfields housing development.

The footpath by Marston's Mill at Earsham, c. 1900. The mill has been redeveloped in recent years for light industry and retail use.

The forge at the top of Hollow Hill, Ditchingham, with the Draper's Lane junction on the right, c. 1900. The road is now the busy Bungay-Norwich B1332 route, and the forge building, though not the business, is still there.

An 1830 painting of Beccles, depicting the market with stalls, traders and shoppers.

The Bungay Horse Fair was an annual event well into the present century. Held at the Fairstead Meadow (now called Skinner's Meadow), in St John's Road, it attracted dealers and farmers (and thieves) from a wide area. Sir Alfred Munnings, the noted horse painter, painted scenes there around the turn of the century. This picture is from around 1940. Today the site is still an open grazing meadow.

Eight
Public Events and Celebrations

Over the centuries local communities have responded to national occasions, and particularly royal occasions, by organizing their own celebrations and festivities or, in the case of sad events, their own tributes. Down the years in Bungay and Beccles and their surrounding villages, there have been many of these to mark accessions, jubilees, coronations, important national dates or the deaths of monarchs. Those organizing them in the Waveney Valley have made them colourful events in which everyone could join, whether they be street parties, festive parades, bonfire parties or memorial services.

Bungay's war memorial to those who died in two world wars stands in the centre of the town, in front of St Mary's church. It was originally erected to those who died in the First World War, and the unveiling was a moving event. Here, the Union Jack has just been removed from the memorial as huge crowds listen to the words of the vicar taking the service following the Second World War.

A busy and colourful scene in Station Road, Beccles, in the 1920s, as a parade provides excitement for participants and onlookers alike. The occasion was probably a carnival procession.

Royal events, whether happy or sad, were marked in towns and districts of the kingdom well into this century, often with processions of one sort or another. This procession moving along Smallgate, Beccles, in 1910, was for the funeral of Edward VII. It was led by the Mayor and Corporation.

The scene at the town end of Upper Olland Street, Bungay, at the time of King George V's Silver Jubilee in 1935. The shop under the Wills Woodbine advert was the shop and tea rooms of baker Mr A.J. Cook (it is now a hair salon). On the left is Mr Harry Ward standing outside his fruit shop, which is now part of Weaver and Dye's electrical goods shop.

Battle of Britain Week was celebrated in uninhibited style all over the country in 1951. There were many activities in Bungay, including street parties, and this one, a children's fancy dress tea party, was in Webster Street, with some eager faces waiting to tuck in.

This impressive bonfire was built at Hall Farm, Mettingham, by this team of adults and children to help celebrate the coronation of King George V in 1911. Ladders were needed to put the flag at the top of the beacon, which is said to have burned well and long.

A procession in Earsham Street, Bungay, with schoolchildren recreating a coronation scene. This was almost certainly 1937 and part of the celebrations at the Coronation of King George VI and Queen Elizabeth.

Fancy dress entries in the Bungay Carnival of 1925. The scene is Wharton Street, beside the ancient almshouses which stood there until demolished in 1930 to make way for the fire station, a building used today as the headquarters for the Bungay St John Ambulance division.

Empire Day, *c.* 1900. Beccles children enjoy a celebration picnic with their teachers and parents on Beccles Common. Each child was given a sticky bun and a cup of lemonade.

The Castle Hills at Bungay were acquired for the town by Bungay Town Trust in 1938. As this poster indicates, a grand fête was held to mark the official opening of them to the public, with money raised by it going towards the cost of buying them, and equipment for them, including children's swings.

BUNGAY CASTLE HILLS

A

GRAND FÊTE

WILL BE HELD IN THE

CASTLE GROUNDS

On Wednesday, 15th June, 1938

to be opened at 2.45 p.m. by

THE COUNTESS OF STRADBROKE, D.B.E.

who will also at 4.30 p.m.

declare Open to the Public
THE CASTLE HILLS

STALLS ⬥ SIDE-SHOWS

IN THE CASTLE GROUNDS

ENTERTAINMENTS

BY PUPILS OF THE VARIOUS SCHOOLS

TEAS WILL BE PROVIDED AT THE CASTLE HILLS

AT REASONABLE PRICES, DURING WHICH

ENTERTAINMENTS WILL BE GIVEN

Admission to Fete, FREE
Admission to Entertainment by Programme:
Adults, 6d.   Children with Adults, 3d.
(If purchased before 15th June: Adults 4d. Children 2d.)

Proceeds for the Purchase and Equipment of the Castle Hills.

A busy scene in New Market, Beccles, in the days before the First World War, with the Barsham Brass Band marching into town as adults and schoolchildren congregate. The rooflines of the buildings have change little in almost ninety years since then, though the shops at ground level have been altered. The occasion could be the accession of King George V in 1910.

The wide spaces in New Market were ideal gathering points in Beccles to celebrate national events. This one was to mark another royal occasion – the Coronation of King George V in 1911. Note the sections chalked on the road surface to indicate where the boys and girls should form up separately.

This pavilion was in the paddock at Valley Farm, Mettingham. The flag decorations suggest this group of ladies could have been celebrating the Coronation of King George VI in 1937, with Mrs Welham, of the Tally Ho! pub, fourth from the left and Mrs Tilney the left-hand lady of the two standing furthest forward.

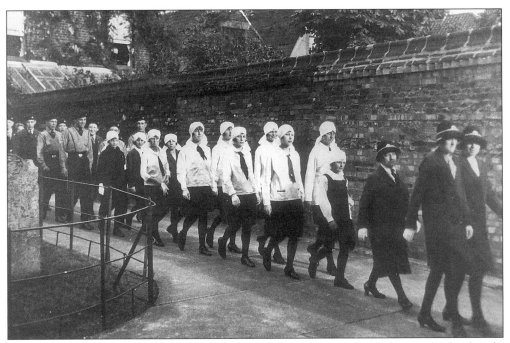

The St George's Day parade in the 1920s, approaching the main door of St Michael's church. The uniforms of the Scouts, Guides and nursing cadets were the fashion of the times.

Woolworth's sixpence bazaar features prominently in the background to this happy occasion – the parade in Beccles town centre to celebrate the coronation of King George VI in 1937.

Flags and bunting bedeck Lower Olland Street, Bungay, as people young and old enjoy a street party. The banner over the street, just seen in the background, says 'Long May they Reign' – the party was to mark the accession to the throne of King George VI and Queen Elizabeth in 1936.

Nine
Railways

The railway system spread its tracks throughout East Anglia in the second half of the nineteenth century, reaching Beccles in the mid-century period and Bungay in the early 1860s. Its coming, followed by the internal combustion engine around the turn of the century, led eventually to the decline in river traffic, and the Waveney Valley line, linking Tivetshall and Beccles via Earsham, Bungay, Ditchingham, Ellingham, and Geldeston, was in its heyday in the first half of this century. There are many today who fondly remember the family outings, or Sunday school outings, to the seaside at Lowestoft or Yarmouth, on the trains drawn by steam locomotives.

Beccles was always on the main Ipswich to Lowestoft line and passenger traffic through it continues today, but Bungay station closed to passenger traffic in 1953, after ninety years' service, and to freight traffic a few years later. It was the end of the era of the branch line, and in 1983 the track disappeared as the Bungay bypass was opened along the same route, to carry modern motor traffic.

The busy scene outside Bungay station in 1910, with carriages waiting to take passengers to their homes, place of work or hotel, and the Great Eastern Railway Company's open top buses providing a connection to other destinations for which Bungay was the nearest railway station.

The staff of Bungay railway station lined up in front of the Great Eastern Railway Company's open top bus outside the station, c. 1910, with passengers looking on from the top. The wooden station buildings seen here were replaced with brick buildings in 1930.

An exterior view of Beccles railway station, *c.* 1910. The station building has changed somewhat, but the basic shape remains the same. Today it is the home of Gifana Reproduction Furniture.

When the age of steam and travel by rail were at their height, pretty well every station of any size had its Smith's bookstall, where you got your paper or magazine to read on your journey, cigarettes or tobacco, and sweets and comics for the children. This one is at Beccles, seen in around 1910, and was on the left facing the platform after you went through the main doors into the station from Station Square. Today those doors are the entrance to the Gifana Reproduction Furniture premises.

The Great Eastern Railway Company staff assembled for a photograph at Beccles station, c. 1900.

A train standing in Beccles station in the early part of the century (pre-1914).

Bombs being unloaded from rail trucks at Earsham station during the Second World War. They were probably bound for the American bomber group based at nearby Flixton airfield – one of the many built in flat East Anglia.

Building work in progress on the construction of the last swing bridge built on the Beccles to Aldeby line. This was one of a series of official railway company photographs taken to record the various stages of the work, and is dated 17 September 1925. The bridge has long since been demolished.

This express train, as they were called in the 1950s when this picture was taken, is standing at the Lowestoft-Ipswich platform at Beccles station. Such locomotives were seldom seen on the Waveney Valley branch line to Bungay, which is the line on the left in this picture. The passenger service on the Waveney Valley branch line closed in 1953, and it was closed to goods traffic in 1963. The busy Bungay bypass now runs along the route of the line.

A passenger train steaming through Ditchingham station, *c.* 1950.

A busy scene at Bungay station, with one goods train (class J150 6-0 No. 65433) passing the signal box, and another (B124-6-0 No. 61577) shunting into the sidings. This scene, from around 1950, clearly shows the train shed where engines were sometimes parked overnight.

A passenger train standing beside the platform at Bungay station, on the Waveney Valley line, c. 1950. The ticket office, waiting room and porters' and stationmaster's office is on the right. The passenger service on the line closed in 1953.

Beccles station, with the Ipswich train standing at the platform. Pictured in the early 1960s, it was the first diesel train to run on the line.

Mr Pettingill, signalman at Beccles station during the 1950s, lovingly tends his flowerbeds on the platform there. In those days awards were made by British Rail for the best kept stations and this was always in the running on the Ipswich-Lowestoft line. The centre line here was the one for London, the line going off to the right was the Waveney Valley branch line to Bungay, and the one on the left was to Lowestoft.

Ten

The River Waveney and Floods

The River Waveney flows from its source at Lopham and Redgrave Fen near Diss to the sea via Breydon Water at Yarmouth, forming the border between Norfolk and Suffolk for the whole of its length. Beccles and Bungay are considered its two twin towns, overlooking its beautiful valley, and their inhabitants make full use of its recreational facilities for fishing, boating, swimming, or walking along its peaceful banks.

The river was navigable to Bungay until 1933, and during the eighteenth and nineteenth centuries water-borne trade brought the town great prosperity. At Beccles holiday cruisers still moor up in large numbers during the summer to enjoy the town and its facilities, making the river one of its greatest assets.

But with its broad flood plain and water meadows, flooding is a regular feature of the area. No winter passes without the meadows being under water for some periods, and in extreme cases, as in 1912 and 1947, homes and businesses can become flooded and roads become impassable. It is one of the drawbacks of living beside a river, but serious flooding is relatively rare, and the compensations of the picturesque Waveney far outweigh these handicaps.

The steam barge *Jeanie Hope* moored at Beccles, around 1900, beside the premises of Nathaniel Walter Pells, miller and merchant. In the background is one of the sailing wherries which plied their trade on the Waveney between Yarmouth and Beccles, and up to Bungay while the river was still navigable. Navigation to Bungay closed in 1933.

This scene is on the River Waveney at Beccles, *c.* 1900, with four swimmers displaying their physique on board a moored yacht. The posers of Victorian times, perhaps!

THE BATHING PLACE, BECCLES.

The Bathing Place in the River Waveney off Puddingmoor, Beccles, *c.* 1910. It was a part of the river partitioned off to form an open-air swimming pool with changing facilities. The present Beccles heated outdoor swimming pool, constructed on rafts, was provided in its place about thirty years ago.

There has been a Beccles Regatta longer than most people can remember and its origins certainly go back to the nineteenth century. This is a busy River Waveney scene during one of the regatta activities in around 1900, with many boats apparently congregating for a parade of decorated vessels, and some youngsters enjoying a dip.

With Beccles being linked to the Norfolk Broads via the River Waveney, pleasure steamers such as this one, *The Yarmouth Belle*, were popular in summer in the early part of the century. She operated daily trips to and from Yarmouth, and had just picked up passengers at the jetty which was near N.W. Pell's miller's premises.

The famous wherries plied their trade around the Broads and rivers of Norfolk and North Suffolk for centuries. These, pictured with sails furled, are on the River Waveney at Beccles, with Darby's timber and boatbuilding yard in the background. Many were built in the area, and Bungay was famous for providing them with 'new bottoms'.

This was the scene on Earsham Dam, to the west of Bungay, in the 1912 floods, with children and adults alike enjoying a paddle, and a horse-drawn carriage making its way through the water.

The scene on Ditchingham Dam during the floods of August 1912, with children enjoying a paddle as a horse and cart makes its way through the water. The house on the right which it is passing is still standing, but the two beyond were demolished many years ago, and the site is now the garden of Joe and Betty Deacon, who live in the next house along.

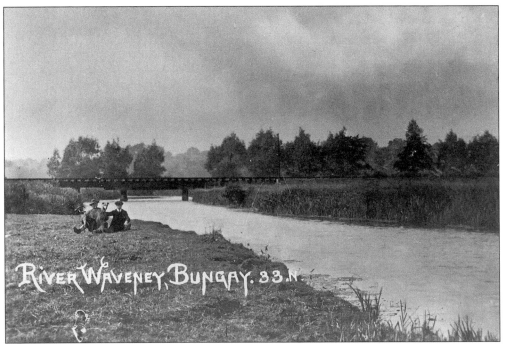

Meadows beside the River Waveney at Bungay, with the railway bridge by Bungay station in the background, *c.* 1930. The road bridge carrying the A143 bypass replaced the rail bridge in 1983.

The extensive floods of 1912 are well documented and are still talked about by older inhabitants of the Waveney Valley. This picture shows a man rowing on the floodwater at Gillingham Dam on 27 August 1912.

Flooding at Bridge Street, Beccles, with children standing bare-legged in the water, 28 August 1912. The onlookers are congregated at the Fen Lane junction, which leads to the River Waveney.

Frozen flood water on Gillingham Dam, just outside Beccles, provided a tempting opportunity for skating, as this picture of around 1910 shows. The meadows flooded regularly. With colder winters in those days, chances to try out the ice happened more regularly than today.

Severe flooding came to the Waveney Valley in 1947, with many homes and buildings affected. This is Ditchingham Dam, just on the Norfolk side of the river and in front of the Falcon public house, with a horse and cart making its way through the flood water.

More floods. This was Wainford Road, Bungay, beside the maltings, c. 1958, after heavy rain had caused the River Waveney by the Three Bridges (in the background) to overflow. These cyclists seem to be making light of it.

The scene at Aldeby swing bridge on the railway line between Beccles and Aldeby during the dramatic floods of 27 August 1912.

Bungay hay maker Charles Hancy brings his horse and cart into action to transport motorcycles and their riders through the floods from Bungay to Ditchingham in 1947.

Eleven

Industry

One of the major industries for both Beccles and Bungay is book printing. Clays (the St Ives Group) in Bungay and William Clowes in Beccles both date back to the nineteenth century. They became flourishing businesses because they were able to provide cheaper labour than in the cities, and had good transport by river and rail. Clays in particular continues to flourish as one of the world's largest book producers and a major employer in the region.

Smaller industries in the past included malting, carriage making and iron founding. Some of these old family industries have continued to prosper, notably Nursey and Son, manufacturers of sheepskin and leather products, which go all over the world. The river trade, with the transport of goods by wherry, was important for the area in the nineteenth century. Unfortunately the river near Bungay had silted up and became impassable for navigation by the 1930s. In Beccles, the waterways continue to flourish as part of the Broads network, attracting tourist cruiser trade in the summer months. Bungay has also suffered as a result of the closure of its railway line in 1953, whereas the Beccles train service has survived, albeit now on a single line track. Following the decline of some local industries, the tourist trade is now of increasing importance to both towns. In this respect, Bungay enjoys a larger number of outstanding historical sites to attract visitors.

The Waveney Valley also functions as an agricultural area, and many of its inhabitants are still employed in growing fruit and vegetables and the rearing of livestock, despite the onset of farming technology. It is this area which creates the special flavour of life in the region. The towns are in close proximity to the beautiful undulating countryside, and the country dwellers rely on the towns for their everyday services and provisions.

Richard Clay (The Chaucer Press) has been Bungay's biggest employer throughout this century. At its height the factory at Broad Street employed over 1,000 people, though today the number is just 450, thanks largely to computer technology. This picture was taken in the linotype department in the 1940s. On the right at the front is Leslie Reeve, father of the compilers of this book.

Delf's Garage was established in Northgate, Beccles, in the early part of this century, and there is still a garage on the site today. The garage staff are pictured here outside the premises, c. 1925.

This group of men are posed around a carrier containing osiers for basket-making. The picture may be at Tivetshall station, on the old Waveney Valley branch line, with Mr Markwell, who ran a basket-making business in Beccles, there to take the consignment home. He is standing with the stationmaster, in his official stationmaster's peaked cap.

Mr Whiteland's oil cart pictured in Broad Street, Bungay, near the printing works, *c.* 1920. It was a familiar sight in the town and district, as was the motor van which succeeded it in the 1950s, dispensing oil and paraffin for lamps, and other household wares. His premises were at 39 Broad Street, near the Horse and Groom pub (now the Green Dragon).

The horse-drawn delivery cart of H. Lawrence and Sons, producers and sellers of mineral waters at Beccles. Their premises were off Station Road. Joe Lawrence, a grandson of the founder of the company, was a school friend of Terry Reeve, co-compiler of this book.

This driver seated on a covered cart drawn by two white horses is pictured outside Crisp's Maltings in Gosford Road, Beccles, c. 1910. He was probably making a delivery of barley or another commodity to the premises. The maltings building has recently been demolished.

A typical building site picture in the early 1900s. This gang of men were working at Earsham, it is believed on a house which now stands adjacent to The Street near the entrance to the present village hall. The bricks may well have come from the local brickworks at Hedenham.

Captain Saunders built an aeroplane works and established the Saunders Aeroplane Company on land near Beccles Common. This is one of its products, made in 1909.

The scene of a dramatic fire at the huge maltings building at Gosford Road, Beccles, in 1912. The fierce blaze completely destroyed the roof and much of the interior of the building, as the crowds gathered to watch. Note the men of the Beccles fire brigade in their splendid uniforms, and the steam pumps used to tackle the blaze.

The Elliott and Garrood factory and iron foundry in Gosford Road, Beccles, c. 1900. At its height it had a workforce of hundreds and a group of them are pictured here. Its products were used countrywide, but it closed during the 1930s. Part of the premises still survive and are occupied by a number of small light industries.

The scene at the Bungay Staithe Maltings, *c.* 1910, when the business was run by W.D. and A.E. Walker. At this time a steam cart, in the centre of the picture, had joined the horses and carts as a mode of transport for carrying goods into town, or to and from the wherries that plied their trade up to the staithe from Yarmouth.

Employees at Green and Co.'s carriage works pictured at the premises, *c.* 1900. The works were immediately over the Falcon Bridge at the bottom of Bridge Street, on the left. Most of the buildings have long since been demolished.

The Waveney Cycle Works were almost opposite Green's carriage works on Ditchingham Dam, with the proprietor pictured here standing outside, *c.* 1900. Triumph Cycles and Bowden brakes are advertised. The premises are now a private house.

R.E. Norman's garage, the Watch House Works, at Beccles Road, Bungay, *c.* 1925, with Mr Norman, in flat cap, standing by the left-hand motorcycle. Also with it, far left, is Mr Boyce, while seated on the other vehicle is Mr A. Jordan. The business was later owned by Claude Mayes, who was an agent for Triumph motorcycles, and is now run by Paul Marshall. The petrol sales facility is now Bungay filling station, next door to Marshall's premises.

This unusual-looking vehicle is the Anglian tricar, which was built in Beccles. However, it was not too successful, apparently because the engine was unreliable, and the premises in Newgate, where the car park now is, closed in 1912.

Cameron's iron foundry shop, which fronted the ironworks in Earsham Street, in 1897. It is decked out to mark the Diamond Jubilee of Queen Victoria's accession, with the workers, young and old, assembled for the occasion.

The interior of Cameron's foundry workshop in Earsham Street, Bungay, c. 1890. The man in the bowler hat is Harry Rumsby, and the bearded gentleman in the foreground at the workbench is his father, Nathan Rumsby. The business later became Rumsby's ironworks; today the court of maisonettes the buildings were converted to long after the business closed is called Nathan's Place. Note the coke stoves on the left, which were among the items manufactured at the works.

This picture of employees at the Staithe Maltings at Bungay, armed with their special shovels for spreading the barley, dates from around 1900. The old White Horse pub can just be seen in the background to the right. Those pictured include A. Honeywood, seated on the right.

Botwright's sawmill in Castle Orchard, Bungay, c. 1930, with three employees about to tackle these huge tree trunks.

Bungay retained its original 'plug-in' telephone exchange until the 1960s, when the new automatic exchange was built in Lower Olland Street. It was in premises in St Mary's churchyard to the rear of Warnes corn and seed merchants' store. This picture, from around 1960, shows, left to right, 'hello' operators Sonia Myall, Iris White, Sylvia Knights, Rita Spittles and Joyce Humphrey.

Mr Page at the rear of the King's Head Hotel at Bungay with the horse which used to draw the railway station taxi for the hotel. The carriage is in the background. In the early 1900s the charges were 3d for a hire around town and 6d to be taken out of town.

BEST SILKSTONE.

MANNING CLARKE,
COAL & COKE MERCHANT,
BRIDGE STREET, BUNGAY,

IS acknowledged to be the Best and Cheapest Merchant in the Town and District for Quality, and now wishes to inform the general public that he has been appointed Special Agent for the Best Silkstone Coal from the Best Yorkshire Collieries.

DIRECT FROM THE COLLIERY TO THE HOME.

SPECIAL TERMS FOR TRUCK LOADS.

DELIVERED BY OWN CARTS TO ANY PART.

CLARKE'S COALS—
THEY ALWAYS STAND THE TEST,
AND PEOPLE SAY THEY ARE THE BEST.

BOATS TO LET.

Manning Clarke was a coal and coke merchant in Bridge Street, Bungay, in the early part of the century, bringing in coal by rail direct from the Yorkshire collieries. With premises close to the River Waveney, it is clear from this advert, which probably dates from the early 1920s, he also had boats for hire from the same spot.

For years at the Bungay printing works of Richard Clay, 12.45 p.m. precisely was lunch-time and the sight of workers streaming home through the town to dinner on their bikes was a familiar – and formidable – one. They were summoned back at 1.40 p.m. by the works hooter. This picture is dated 11 September 1959.

Bungay's printing works, Richard Clay (The Chaucer Press), pictured from the Common, c. 1900. The business employed over 1,000 people at one time, but modern computer technology has reduced that to 450 today. Now part of the St Ives Group, Bungay produced books to go all over the world.

Another commercial delivery vehicle familiar around the streets and roads of Bungay and district in the early part of the century. Cocks and Son, drapers, had their shop in Earsham Street, where it also ran a grocery store. Note the telephone number on the van: 7.

Charles Marston ran mills at Bungay, Earsham and Harleston. This is one of his Garrett steam wagons, pictured near the Earsham mill, with Earsham church visible on the left, in 1920. Jack Mayhew is the stoker, and driver George Wilby can just be seen at the wheel.